D0978291

A Western Reprint

LADIES WERE NOT EXPECTED

Abigail Scott Duniway
and Women's Rights

Abigail Scott Duniway, 1871

Dorothy Nafus Morrison

LADIES
WERE NOT
EXPECTED

Abigail Scott Duniway
and Women's Rights

A Western Reprint
from
WESTERN IMPRINTS
The Press of the Oregon Historical Society
1985

LIBRARY OF CONGRESS CATALOGING IN PUBLICATION DATA

Morrison, Dorothy N   Ladies were not expected.

SUMMARY: A biography of the leader of the women's
suffrage movement in Oregon.
  1.   Duniway, Abigail Scott, 1834–1915—Juvenile
literature.   2.   Feminists—United States—Biography—
Juvenile literature.   3.   Women—Suffrage—United States
—Juvenile literature.   [1.   Duniway, Abigail Scott,
1834–1915.   2.   Feminists.   3.   Women—Suffrage]
I.   Title.
HQ1413.D86M67   324'.3'0924[B] [92]   77–2969
ISBN 0-87595-168-6

First edition (1977) published by Atheneum, New York City
Second edition (1985) published by
WESTERN IMPRINTS
The Press of the Oregon Historical Society

A Western Reprint

To my girls

Anne Lynne Fiona Mary Jenny

who can live more fully
because Abigail and others
fought for "the cause."

Contents

Author's Note

EVERYTHING in this book is true. All the incidents really happened, just as I have told them, and all the conversations were really spoken. Most of the dialog is taken verbatim from Abigail's own vivid writings; most briefer quotes are also from her, the rest from her family and friends, or from publications of her time. In a few pages I have turned indirect quotes into direct ones. Abigail was a writer, and a good one. It was not necessary to invent passages, when her own were at hand.

I wish to thank Janice Worden, Elizabeth Winroth, and all the staff of the Oregon Historical Society for willing and expert assistance in locating material, and for the use of their extensive collections. I also wish to thank the staff of the Multnomah County Library, who have been unfailingly kind.

Helen Krebs Smith, author of the Duniway biography, *Presumptuous Dreamers*, has been generous in sharing her impressive research. Elesa Scott Keeney, granddaughter of Harvey Scott, furthered my insight into the relationship between her grandfather and Abigail. Jean Ward of Lewis and Clark College furnished certain letters. Ruth Stoller oriented me to historic Lafayette. I am grateful to all of these.

And most especially I want to thank David C. Duniway, grandson of Abigail. He gave me interviews, let me study family papers, permitted the use of family pictures, and granted the right to use quotes from the Trail Diary. He read the manuscript and made many suggestions. He is a trained historian, and his treasured advice has been more helpful than I can possibly say.

LADIES
WERE NOT
EXPECTED

Abigail Scott Duniway
and Women's Rights

String Bean

1834–1852

I WEPT bitterly when you were born."

Abigail Scott's mother said it so quietly that Abigail wasn't sure she had heard it right. She had been enjoying this special chance for them to talk together on her tenth birthday, but now she was puzzled. She smoothed her long skirts and watched her mother's sad face.

"You cried?" Abigail asked. "Why?"

"Because you were a girl."

"And Pa?"

"He was cross."

As Abigail folded and unfolded her thin hands, she remembered the day Sarah Mariah had been born, for her mother had wept then, too, and murmured, "Poor Baby! Poor little

Jenny's mother, Anne Roelofson Scott.

Jenny's father, John Tucker Scott.

thing!" She remembered the day John came, when everyone was full of joy.

At that moment, Abigail understood that her father would always be proud to have a boy, her mother would always be glad. But when a girl was born, he would be cross, and her mother would weep.

Then she hadn't been wanted, either. Because she was a girl, she had been "a grievance almost too burdensome to be borne."

She never forgot the hurt.

ABIGAIL had been born on October 22, 1834, on a farm in Illinois, the second child in the family. Although her name was really Abigail Jane, everyone called her Jenny.

Her father was John Tucker Scott, a huge, stern man with hawklike nose, not unkind, but too strong to realize how tired others might feel. "Hard work never hurt anybody," was a common saying then, and Tucker Scott put it into practice. Intelligent—demanding—unyielding—he ruled the family with a hand of granite. Although Jenny loved him, she resented him too.

When she was a baby, her grandmother Roelofson was hurt in a fall, so Jenny's meek, sweet-tempered, frail mother tried to manage both households. Baby Jenny often sat on the floor, crying but neglected, soothed only by a piece of bacon attached by a string to a bedpost, while house flies swarmed around her.

7

Although Jenny's mother soon had only her own home to manage, the family became unsettled again because Tucker Scott cosigned some notes with his younger brother, Lindsey. When Jenny was about four, her Uncle Lindsey "fell into evil ways," went out drinking with some friends, committed a minor crime, and was whipped to death by a mob.

This tragedy shattered the whole family, and of course little Jenny heard much about it. For Tucker Scott it meant disaster, because when the notes fell due, he had to pay them. As a result he lost his farm and moved his family to the small town of Wesley, Illinois.

There he ran the first circular sawmill west of the Ohio River. To a child this was a wonderful machine, powered by horses that plodded around and around a circle. Moreover, it prospered, which allowed Tucker Scott to rebuild his fortunes. Finally Grandfather Scott built himself a small house, and Jenny's parents moved into the "big house" on the home-

The Scott farm near Groveland, Illinois.

stead, with its wide lawn and shade trees. This was the childhood home that Jenny remembered best.

Beautiful as it was, the farm meant endless work. A new baby came almost every year, although three died young. Each one meant more food to raise, more meals to cook over an open fire, more clothing and blankets to spin and weave and sew.

Right from the start, Jenny had to work hard. While still so small she had to stand on a chair to reach the table, she washed stacks of dishes. Instead of a sink she had only a couple of big pans, and a bar of strong homemade soap that made her hands sting.

She pared, cored, and quartered heaps of apples, which she threaded on long strings to be hung up and dried for the winter's pies and sauce. She sat for hours with a lapful of prickly wool fleece, going over it inch by inch to pull out burrs and seeds so it could be spun. The monotonous jobs often confined her from daylight to dark.

One summer, when Jenny was only nine, she had to resod the lawn, which had been damaged by drought. This meant hacking at the tough sod, prying it off, and lifting it in chunks.

Tucker Scott might believe that hard work never hurt anyone, but when Jenny tackled this, she injured her back and never fully recovered.

She grew into a tall, spindly, frail stringbean 11 of a girl, often a rebel. She churned, scrubbed clothes on a washboard, spun, gathered wood, and carried buckets of sap for the maple sugar camp. She milked cows, hoed fields, dragged dead limbs from the trees nearby and chopped them for firewood.

One spring she and her brother Harvey, three years younger, were supposed to plant a ten-acre cornfield, but they grew so tired, they rebelled and skipped an island in the center. When the corn came up, their stern father noticed the bald place.

"You did it on purpose?" he demanded, and red-faced and ashamed, they had to confess.

Even though Jenny loved books and wanted to learn, she was frail and often too ill to attend the log school with her brothers and sisters, so her busy mother somehow found time to teach her to read, spell and recite rhymes. She also went for five months to what she called "an apology for an academy," something like a modern high school. She began to write "poesy," and the whole family was proud when some of her verses were published in the county newspaper.

For a while a thin-faced, long-legged minister named Reverend Lawrence boarded at the Scott home. Jenny and her sisters, who were never happy about extra work, didn't like waiting on him. Jenny tartly called him "a milk and water specimen of humanity." However, he did them one good turn, for he subscribed to the *New York Tribune,* a famous antislavery newspaper edited by Horace Greeley.

Although Tucker Scott was strongly opposed to slavery, he didn't approve of the *Tribune,* which he considered radical. When he saw it in his own home, he was furious.

"An incendiary abolitionist affair!" he roared, and forbade the children to read it. After that, naturally, Jenny would watch her chance, carry it off, and devour every word.

Later, when her father changed his mind about the *Tribune,* Jenny read Greeley's paper regularly. "He did more to shape my destiny than anyone else," she said. She dreamed that some day she might "see him in the flesh and shake his hand."

Uprooted

1852

A T SEVENTEEN Jenny was tall and thin, pale, not really pretty except for her sparkling blue eyes. Life crackled around her, because she had a tart tongue and vivid imagination. She was strong-willed, gloriously happy or fiercely indignant or lost in despair.

Covered wagons of emigrants on their way to Missouri and the Oregon Trail often passed the family farm, and many nights barefoot children of the wagoners came to the door of Jenny's home, carrying hickory or walnut sticks, asking for coals. Her mother would give them a few from the fire that was always kept going in the fireplace.

The emigrants talked about leaping salmon and rich deep soil in the Oregon Territory, where land was free for the taking, where it never snowed. Jenny's father knew some of the important men among the early emigrants, and the Scott family had relatives in Oregon who 14 wrote them long, rosy letters. A faraway look came into Tucker Scott's eyes when the wagon trains passed, and one day he said they were to go too.

Jenny's mother wept and protested, but he was the law. None of the family dreamed of refusing to do as they were told. Instead, the mother and daughters worked all winter making a store of bedding and blankets, stockings and sunbonnets, hickory shirts and gingham aprons. It was a sorrowful job. Jenny's sister Kitty wrote of tears that fell upon the garments, of fingers that trembled as they stitched and knitted and wove by the flickering light of tallow candles.

In early spring Tucker Scott told the family how little they could take along. "Nothing worth less than a dollar a pound," he said.

He sold his interest in the farm, sold his stock, and had an auction for most of their household goods. Jenny and the others watched while their cherished bureaus and chests, carpets, most of their pots and pans and dishes,

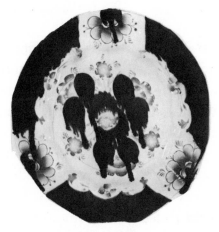

One of the Dutch plates lovingly
smuggled to Oregon in a feather bed.

even their precious few books, were held up for everyone to see and buy.

One of their treasures was a set of six bright-colored Dutch plates, dark blue on white, with a gaudy design of pink flowers. When the auctioneer came to these, a young man named George, who was going with Jenny's older sister Fanny, bought them.

"For you, Fanny," he said, handing them over.

Fanny wanted to take them along. They all did. Surprisingly, Jenny's meek little mother turned smuggler.

"We'll do it," she decided.

"But how? Pa won't let us."

"There's a way."

Their mother helped Fanny sew the plates into the very feather bed that Tucker Scott himself would sleep on, packing them so well they wouldn't be crushed.

Jenny also had a treasure, a blue-backed spelling book, small and battered, but holding hundreds of words that she longed to learn. She couldn't bear to leave it behind.

So, being Jenny, she tucked it into the bottom of her sewing bag, well covered with scraps, where nobody would see it. Words were priceless, she thought. You could do anything with words.

Having nine children, Tucker Scott organized them as a general would marshal his army. The older girls, Fanny, who was eighteen, fifteen-year-old Maggie, and thirteen-year-old Kitty, were to help with the cooking and washing. Etty, age eleven, was to ride behind the train on the pony Shuttleback and bring up any cattle that might stray, while Harvey, age fourteen, was to drive. The little ones, John, Sarah Mariah, and three-year-old Willie, who was everyone's darling, would be passengers.

Jenny thought she had the finest job of all.

17

Jenny's sisters, Etty, Kitty and Maggie, in a photograph taken approximately 1852.

Since her verses had been published, she was to keep the trail diary. Her father gave her a special ledger for it, covered with marbleized paper all brown and gold, with a brown leather spine.

18   Tucker Scott had planned well. He had a full two thousand dollars in cash, plenty of oxen, several horses, three cows, and five heavy, springless wagons with strong canvas tops. Rifles hung from leather straps; goods were stored in boxes and bundles. He had hired several drivers, including John McDonald, twenty-one years old, from a nearby town. In addition, seventeen other adults had joined the party, with twenty-two more wagons. It was a strong, well-prepared train.

At last, on April 2, they were ready to leave, and the blue-backed speller was still safe in Jenny's workbag. Family and friends gathered weeping as Jenny and her mother and sisters embraced each one, then climbed into place.

Their grandfather was there, the grandfather on whose land they had lived so long. He was weeping too, and waving his red handkerchief. As the wagons rumbled away from the farm, the last things Jenny saw were the flash of red, grandfather's gray hair blowing in the breeze, and the soft spring snowflakes falling over all.

CHAPTER THREE

The Crossing

1852

THE long trip meant freedom for Jenny, release from drudgery. At first keeping the journal was fun. While her mother and sisters did the camp cooking, she sat down happily with her pen and ink, composing it with care, searching for just the right words. No telling who might read it some day.

But the writing soon turned into a dreaded chore, for her father supervised every entry, told her what to include, made sure she had correct mileage and locations for every single camp. She put it off, protested, sometimes refused until he gave her "a box on the ear," or grimly wrote it up himself.

She reveled in the excitement of the trail. When a storm blew over a tent, she described

Arrival of a Ship to Oregon

April 2nd; leaving home, home, friends and home associates in
old Daywell, as are this evening snugly quartered in
the open prairie 15 miles from Peoria and 9 miles
from Farmington; have had but little difficulty in
our journey so far; crossed the Illinois river (probably
the last time) with but little difficulty and in a word
had had no trouble at all except what has been
occasioned by bidding farewell forever to those
with whom most of us have associated all
our lives; and to me it was a great thing (to leave
the home of my childhood, the place where, when
a care to me, was a stranger, I was sent to roam
over hill and dale and when ashes I came to

The first page of the Journal entrusted to Abigail on the trip west.

"the many laughs and jests occasioned by the predicament the inmates of the tent were left in for a few moments."

They had breakfast in a snowstorm with "our victuals, crusted (not with sugar) but snow."

In Missouri she was shocked at seeing slaves.

"May none of *us* ever be guilty of buying and selling the souls and bodies of our fellow creatures; slavery is a withering blight upon the prospects, happiness and freedom of our Nation."

She had her share and more of adventures. At famous Independence Rock she and her sisters lingered to climb it. By the time they had ascended thirty feet, hail and wind drove them off, and when they hurried back to camp, they found that their father had started to cross the Sweetwater River. They ran their fastest, overtaking the train just in time to jump aboard the last wagon. Stormy as it was, Tucker Scott had intended to let them wade the waist-deep stream, to teach them not to get so far behind.

Jenny had a way of shrugging off punishments. "I would have liked the fun of wading well enough," she wrote, "but did not like to get joked about being left."

She wandered over the flower-strewn prairies. Once she didn't overtake the wagons until ten o'clock. Another day, when she and Kitty went ahead to escape the dust, they kept on for two miles beyond the stopping point, and had   23 to walk back through the dark forest. They were met first by Harriet, searching for them on the faithful horse Sukey, and then by their father, who was "quite out of patience."

Jenny's shoes had long ago been replaced by moccasins, whose soles she now wore off completely, hurrying back. And still she could tell of "our ludicrous mistake at least we considered it ludicrous when we got time to laugh."

According to her sisters, the young driver John McDonald was "sweet on" Jenny. Although she didn't mention it in writing, that would add to the excitement of the trail.

Some pages of the diary were streaked with tears, for the emigrants sickened with cholera. On June 20, near Fort Laramie in Wyoming, Jenny wrote:

"How mysterious are the works of an all-wise and overruling Providence! We little thought when last Sabbath's pleasant sun shed upon us his congenial rays that when the next

24

Independence Rock, which Jenny and her sisters tried to climb before being driven off by hail and wind.

An emigrant camp on the Oregon Trail. In her Journal Jenny wrote: "We have a fair specimen here tonight of the various occupations of different persons in the world. Betting and playing cards is going on at one encampment, music and dancing at another, while at a third persons are engaged in singing religious hymns and psalms with apparent devotion. Indians of the Shoshonee tribe are encamped near us in several wigwams."

25

should come it would find us mourning over the sickness and death of our beloved Mother!"

The illness had struck with terrifying speed. One day Jenny's mother seemed as well as usual. The next, she was gone. The next, they held an early-morning graveside service, on a mountain slope beside a spring, with wild roses blooming nearby.

"We this morning dispatched our breakfast in silence and with sorrowful hearts prepared to pay the last tribute of respect to the remains of our beloved lamented dead."

They had no coffin. Instead, they scooped out a grave in the soft sandstone, and that same day the train moved on, traveling twenty miles.

Cattle also died. The wagon carrying the girls overturned, but no one was hurt. They forded rivers, went up and down steep slopes, struggled through quicksand.

When the herd stampeded across a river, John McDonald and another young man tried to follow, and in the swift current John was drowned. This was a special blow to Jenny. In the battered, ink-spattered diary she wrote:

"I am seated in the same place where I was when writing last evening but alas! how

changed are our prospects, how greatly changed
are meditations! The roaring of the river is no
longer pleasant music to my ears, but is a jar-
ring discordant sound, and I startle and half rise
to my feet at rustling of the leaves about me; 27
and these huge rocks which I then looked upon
with admiration, now only terrify me . . . "

On August 28, tragedy struck still again.
"The ruthless monster death not yet content,
has once more entered our fold & taken in his
icy grasp the treasure of our hearts! Last night
our darling Willie was called from earth, to vie
with angels around the throne of God."

The grave beside the trail was a tiny one,
hard to leave alone in the empty land.

By the time they began the roughest stretch
of all, over the Cascade Mountains, their food
was nearly gone. Jenny's Uncle Levi Caffee pretended to look forward to it.

"Ten days on half allowance and two weeks
without anything to eat!" he said. "Lawd,
Lawd, the prospect tickles me!"

Day after day they lurched over the mountain trail. Jenny and her sisters found salal berries to eat, but there wasn't even a cup of coffee
grounds in camp, and Uncle Levi was hungry.
Recklessly Jenny stood in front of him, hands

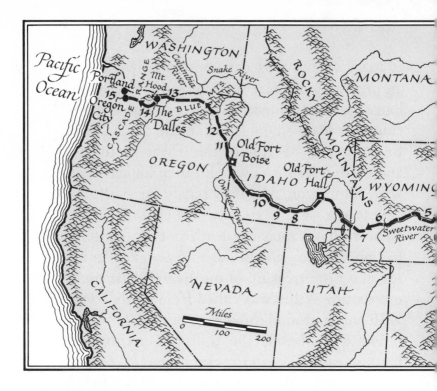

Legend

1. *Friday, April 2. Leave farm two miles south of Groveland, Ill.*

2. *Thursday, April 15, near Lewistown in Lewis County, Mo. Sees slaves.*

3. *Sunday, May 30. Ford Platte River. Quicksand in river. Most wagon trains traveled on the south side of the Platte, but Tucker Scott led his people along the north side.*

4. *Sunday, June 20. Mother dies, two miles southeast of Cassa, on north side of the Platte River, 31 miles northwest of Fort Laramie.*

5. *Tuesday, June 29, to Sweetwater River, near Independence Rock. This is the rock Jenny and her sisters climbed and were forced to leave because of the storm. They barely caught up with the wagon train before they crossed the Sweetwater. Her father was going to let them wade to teach them a lesson.*

6. *Sunday, July 4. In Antelope Hills a storm upsets two tents and makes the wagons rock from side to side.*

7. *Tuesday, July 6. Enter "Old Oregon"—Oregon Territory—in Wyoming, at Pacific Springs.*

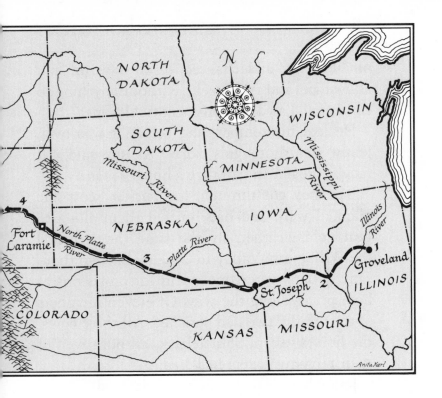

8. *Friday, July 23, at Fort Hall. Fanny's shoes give out completely, and she has to cover her feet with wrappings as best she can.*

9. *Saturday, July 24. Ford the Portneuf River. Five miles northeast of American Falls the wagon carrying the girls upsets in a mud hole, but the girls are not hurt.*

10. *Friday, July 30, on the Snake River, in Idaho. John McDonald is drowned when the stock stampede across the river.*

11. *August 28. Willie dies, near Durkee, Oregon.*

12. *Saturday, September 4. Kitty and Jenny walk ahead and the train stops behind them. They have to walk back through the intense darkness of the forest.*

13. *Friday, September 17, the Dalles, Oregon. Tucker Scott buys his daughters shoes.*

14. *Monday, September 20, the Barlow Road, over the Cascade Mountains. Jenny teases her Uncle Levi, to her regret.*

15. *The settlement in Oregon City, in Willamette Valley, near the relatives' home.*

on her hips, and chanted, "Ten days on half allowance, and two weeks without anything to eat! Lawd, Lawd, the prospect tickles me!"

He lost his temper, and before it was over, 30 Jenny was thoroughly sorry. As she said, "It taught me not to tantalize a hungry man."

But they got through, for Tucker Scott had planned well, and had hurried them along to beat cold weather. By the time they reached the Willamette Valley in Oregon, his two thousand dollars were gone, spent for provisions at high prices along the way. Of eleven members of the family, two had perished. All three cows, the horses except Shuttleback, all but seven of their forty-two oxen, had died.

Jenny herself had grown and changed.

She had tasted freedom from drudgery.

She had earned her way with her pen.

She had seen her mother die, a helpless passenger on a journey she made against her will, because her husband said she must.

Hardscrabble

1852–1857

THE Willamette River flows north in Oregon, through a valley that is fifty or more miles wide in places, with the Cascade Mountains to the east, the Coast Range to the west. When Jenny came, much of the valley was a natural rolling prairie, dim and green in the misty fall rains, with scattered stands of fir and oak. Smaller streams flowed down from the mountains into the Willamette, and beside one of these, the Yamhill, huddled the tiny frontier town of Lafayette.

Here Jenny and her family spent that first winter. Tucker Scott, his money gone, rented a primitive building and started a hotel which he called the Oregon Temperance House. Since the temperance movement, which asked for restraint in the use of liquor, was strong in the West, the hotel was generally well filled.

Too well, Jenny thought. She and her sisters were trapped again, cooking and cleaning, not for the family this time, but for her father's boarders.

However, she had gained confidence. She was quick-witted, had had verses published, and had kept a trail diary for a whole summer. So she managed to get a job as teacher in a log school in the tiny nearby town of Cincinnati, now known as Eola. It wasn't easy to keep ahead of her pupils in such subjects as grammar and advanced arithmetic, which she had never studied, but she loved it. Head high, she swept her long skirts across the board walks of the little town, back and forth from boarding house to school. The blue-backed speller, which had come safely through, was useful now.

In the Oregon Territory a man who came before December 1, 1850, could claim three hundred and twenty acres, or if he came within the next three years he could have one hundred and sixty. In either case, if he married soon enough, his wife could claim a like amount in her own name. So women of any age were prizes. Hopeful bachelors, trudged from cabin to cabin, knocking politely on the doors and asking whether any unmarried females lived there.

Jenny, with her flashing blue eyes and smooth young face, soon had dozens of suitors among the brawny, sun-tanned ranchers and lumberjacks.

Eighteen by now, she made a good choice in Ben Duniway, four years older. He was a dark-eyed, good-natured fellow who had come with the emigrants of 1850, had worked in the mines for a season, and was preparing to claim a homestead.

Jenny remembered so vividly the tragedy of her mother's life that she deleted "obey" from the marriage service, with Ben's amiable consent. She also refused to take a land claim, for she scorned the idea of "land brides"—girls whose husbands mainly wanted their land. If Ben wished to marry her, let him prove he was doing it for herself alone!

The record book of donation land claims bears a heavy black entry beside Ben's name: "Wife Not Entitled." Few claims are marked this way, because most young couples would not pass up free land. But Ben on his own could

34

Fragment of picture showing Ben Duniway with Clara and Willis, probably done around 1857.

take three hundred and twenty acres, so that was the size of their farm.

Jenny, who had dreamed such dreams, soon found herself as caged as her mother had been. Since the best land had been taken early, Ben's farm was in the back woods, tangled and fringed with tall timber. Hardscrabble was the name generally given to that area. Wild animals were troublesome, and money was short. Within a year baby Clara was born, soon followed by a baby boy, Willis.

Ben, sociable and easygoing, still had many bachelor friends.

"Nothing," Jenny later said, "delighted him more than to mobilize them at mealtime at our cabin in the wilderness." Whether she and the babies were well or ill, she had to "feed the crowd to repletion."

Jenny's father soon married the widow of a man who had died on the trail. Big sister Fanny was also married, but Etty lived with the Duniways most of the time, and sometimes Kitty did too.

Even though they helped her, the work was endless. Jenny was cooking for a table of hungry young men, cleaning, baby-tending, washing with scrubboard, spinning and weaving, churning, milking, taking care of chickens. But it was Ben who carried her butter and eggs and candles and soap to town and came home with the money in his pocket.

At that time, in all the Pacific Northwest, no married woman owned any property, except the few who had acquired free land. Even a wedding trousseau, bought for a girl by her father, legally belonged to the husband.

"To make thousands of pounds of butter every year for market," Jenny wrote, "to bake and clean and stew and fry; to be, in short, general pioneer drudge, with never a penny of my own, was not a pleasant business for an erstwhile school teacher."

36   However, Ben was kind, and Jenny had been brought up to believe that hard work and dependence were the heaven-ordained lot of women. She was ashamed of her rebelliousness and kept it hidden.

Sometimes she envied her brother Harvey. He worked hard as rancher, miner or lumberjack, but whenever he had enough money he attended Pacific University for a term or so. Jenny wrote bitterly that if she had been a man she, too, could have had an education and a good job.

Life at Hardscrabble was never easy, but neither was it dull. Once the sky turned dark and was filled with a roaring. Terrified, Jenny covered baby Clara with her own body and crouched in a corner, back to the storm, while the roof, front door, and some of the walls blew off. The house was filled with fence rails, clapboards, firewood, and splinters, until the only free spot was the one where she huddled.

When the wind died, a hailstorm began. In the roofless house Jenny protected baby Clara

Harvey Scott, Jenny's brother, at nineteen.

with a patchwork quilt, and at last, when the hail let up, she waded knee deep through frozen slush to the nearest neighbors.

Pioneers were used to "making do," so Ben soon rebuilt the cabin. But another day he and Jenny, with Clara and the new baby Willis, paid a visit to some friends. When they returned, they found their home a charred ruin, with all their crude bits of furniture and clothing burned. Again neighbors took them in until Ben could provide another shelter.

This gave Jenny a chance to branch out, and she seized it. While living at the neighbor's, she taught a three-month term of school.

For that brief time she had a use for her lively mind. But when the new cabin was ready, she had to return to Hardscrabble.

Scribbling

1857–1859

BACK in her own cabin, Jenny fell ill. It may have been a physical disease or exhaustion or sheer frustration, for she detested housework and farm work and wasn't expert at either one. Whatever the reason, she had to spend hours of every day lying down. To occupy her restless mind, she began to "scribble," and one day when Ben burned a majestic fir tree to clear the land, she wrote a long poem, *The Burning Forest Tree*. At Ben's urging, she copied it carefully on brown wrapping paper, which was all she had, and sent it to the editor of the *Oregon Argus* along with a letter that said:

"I have to write with one foot upon the cradle-rocker; I live upon a farm, cook for work-

The Oregon Argus

—A Weekly News-paper, devoted to the Principles of Jeffersonian Democracy, and advocating the side

Vol. III.   OREGON CITY, OREGON, SEPTEMBER 12, 1857.

☞ The writer of the following says in a private note—"I have to write with one hand upon the cradle-rocker; I live upon a [?], cook for workmen, make a great deal of butter, and tend two babies." A wo- man who can do all this and be sufficiently contented and happy to draw poetry from the surroundings of a home in the timber, must be a wife worth having. Her article has merit, but we cannot depart from our rule again by publishing for her without knowing her real name.

For the Argus.
The Burning Forest Tree.

'Tis night; slowly the orb of day passed through the gold-tinged curtains, grand, and faded from our view. The queenly moon, with pale, calm face,

thorne, cast out from society, and deemed unworthy of the civilities and courtesies of life, yet bearing it all with meekness. "Ah, but there was divinity." I answer, "Be ye perfect, even as your Father which is in Heaven is perfect."   D. B. G.

LINN Co., Aug. 22, 1857.

For the Argus.
Notes from a Traveler's Diary.

Pursuing our course, our way became more and more obstructed, and our trail, which in the beginning was plainly mark- ed, now seemed to have vanished into air, or (more properly speaking) into the

ashamed," &c. I have no idea that any- body but "Reform" ever made any such discovery. I presume, Mr. Editor, I'm about the "same on the "goose" as you are, judging by your remarks, and I have been for many years an observer, to some extent, of men, and to considerable extent on the [?] women, and I have never seen a man who was "ashamed," or "shunned good company," or "sneaked off by himself," to smoke. I have known gentlemen,— those who were considered models of gen- tility in good society,—who both smoked and chewed tobacco, and who never "sneak- ed off by themselves," on account of eith- er. I have known gentlemen to light their cigars, and politely excuse themselves for a

Of tree-frog's wife, as happy now he chants
His evening melody.
One interesting sight
Presents itself to my view, as with
An earnest gaze I look upon its glories
Fast departing.
'Tis an aged tree; perhaps two centuries have
passed
Since first his tiny branches burst
All gladly into life. I dimly scan
The distant years, long, long since fled,
When thou, majestic giant, didst shoot forth
Thy tender limbs to catch the gentle dews
Of heaven. Say, who inhabited the land,
When first the wild dove cooed among thy leaflets?
Who, what race of men did wander round thee,
Gazing with proud fondness on thy well-
Proportioned limbs?
Methinks I hear thy answer; when thy life was
young,
'Twas a race of men who, when thy life was
young,
Were noble, gen'rous, brave. Perchance thou hast,
In days long since gone by, been witness of
Heroic deeds; deeds of those men who like thyself
Are dwindling into dust. May hap a crown
Of thy green twigs has been placed on the brow
Of some dark maiden, who has plighted vows
Of love and honor to her heart's best choice.
Ah! thou hast stood, thro' long and dreary years,
The year of tempests and the chilling blasts
Of dreary winters. Two years ago, and I beheld
thee,
The tall & forest tree within my stale
Of vision; then thou wast in thy glory;
But very soon a mighty whirlwind tore away
Thy top, and spoiled thy matchless grandeur.
Since then
Till now thou hast not been molested,
But hast lain, one half stretched out in death,
Upon thy mother earth, while yet thy trunk

from the labyrinth of fallen timber in which we were entangled. The mountains began to assume a more broken and precipitous appearance, and nature seemed to have lost the bright smiling look she wears where man has made his home.— Discovered a mountain shrub very common in the gold mines of California, in appearance somewhat resembling laurel. There it goes by the name of manzinnets, and I had never seen it or heard it spoken of as existing here. It bears clusters of yellowish red berries, which are sweet and rather pleasant to the taste, though they are as dry as powder inside and may be crumbled to dust in the hand, and blown away by the breath. We also found abundance of sallalberries and red huckleberries, both of an unusual size and fine flavor. We also found a small nut contained in a rough husk or burr, resembling chestnut in appearance and somewhat in taste, and by our guide called chincapin or dwarf chestnut. Straggling along in Indian file, we wore seldom all together, unless the leader was checked by some obstacle, or, as sometimes happened, old Packy lost his balance

ing, of itself, does not show a lack of gentility; but smoking without permission, in the presence of ladies, does. I have known ladies, who could bear neither the smell nor the taste of oyster. Does the gentleman who eats them, show a want of good manners? It certainly would not be proper to set them before a lady, to whom they were known to be offensive; but if the gentleman took his dish of oyster soup, and politely withdrew to another room, he would, according to "Reform," be "sneaking off by himself," or "on the look-out" &c. I am glad to believe, with "Reform," that the number of ladies, who use tobacco, is small; but "Reform" hopes the number will "become more and more less," &c. Beautiful! is'nt it? What would Murray way to that?

And now, Mr. Editor, to conclude, I will say, that if any sensible man will read that part of "Reform's" article beginning at the words, "And now, when about drawing to a close," and read to the next period, and not pronounce the author non compos mentis, I will confess myself deceived. That the use of tobacco is an un-

Section of the front page of *The Oregon Argus*, showing part of "The Burning Forest Tree" by a new young poet Abigail Scott Duniway. The signature, "Jenny Glen" is not visible here.

men, make a great deal of butter, and tend two babies."

She signed her letter, "Jenny Glen."

To her joy, the poem was printed, and soon others were too. But once she was hurt because the editor said he accepted her verse "to please its author."

By the end of 1857, when Jenny was twenty-three, they had lived at Hardscrabble four years, long enough to "prove" Ben's claim, so he bought a better farm, Sunny Hill Side near her first town of Lafayette. However, they didn't as yet sell the Hardscrabble land. At Sunny Hill Side Jenny no longer had to feed the hungry bachelors. Instead she cooked for hired hands. And bore another little son, Hubert.

These were times of upheaval, and people argued out their differences by writing letters to country newspapers. Oregon was about to become a state instead of a territory, so one favorite topic was politics. Another was slavery, for the Civil War was approaching. Still another was women's rights.

When the *Argus* printed some letters about woman's place in the home, Jenny plunged in with a fighting reply that called the others "a mess of abuse," and proudly said, "I am married to a husband who takes care of the baby upon all convenient occasions."

An exciting flurry of letters followed. One writer called Ben "hen-pecked," and said that "Mrs. D. even goes so far as to boast of making a nurse of him." Most writers used false names such as "Xenittie", "Lear", and "Etc.", but Jenny boldly signed her own. Abigail J. Duniway. It looked fine in print. She continued to use Abigail as her professional name, though the family still called her Jenny.

She also wrote a long series of articles for the Oregon Farmer, which she signed "A Farmer's Wife." These were lively, often acid, and so popular that they were listed in the newspaper's yearly index. Young Abigail Duniway was beginning to be famous around the log cabins nearby. Her neighbors would ride for miles to hear her read her latest published piece.

Even though the farm work was still hard, Jenny—Abigail—now was happy, for she was writing, and Ben was "sober, industrious, and kind." He spent hours caring for the children or playing with them. They were "a source of abiding joy."

The year 1859, when Abigail was twenty-five, was a banner one twice over, for Oregon became a state, and she had a book published. It was *Captain Gray's Company, or Crossing*

44

CAPTAIN GRAY'S COMPANY;

OR,

CROSSING THE PLAINS

AND

LIVING IN OREGON.

BY

MRS. ABIGAIL J. DUNIWAY.

" Westward the course of Empire takes its way."

PORTLAND, OREGON:
PRINTED AND PUBLISHED BY S. J. McCORMICK,
1859.

The title page of Abigail Scott Duniway's book, *Captain Gray's Company*, the first novel ever to be printed west of the Rocky Mountains.

the Plains and Living in Oregon—largely the story of her own emigration. Some copies were bound in red cloth, others in green, blue, plum or brown. All had scrolls embossed on the cover and her name in gold on the spine. *Mrs.* 45 *A. J. Duniway.*

Most of its newspaper reviews were bad. "In hastily looking over the pages after the merits we do not find them," said one.

"It is a silly story . . . expressed in bad grammar."

Another, in the *Pacific Christian Advocate,* spoke of "huge disgust" at its love stories and poor grammar. This enraged Abigail so that she dashed off a scorching letter to the reviewer.

"I know your *taste* or *integrity,* but, seriously, I have no respect for either. You 'have been sickened with the love stories' eh? That's a natural consequence to me of *your* temperament and I do not wonder at it in the least . . . I'll remember you in my next public effort in a character that you can't mistake."

In spite of the bad reviews, *Captain Gray's Company* sold fairly well, and it expressed Abigail's ideas, which even then were well formed.

Most of its women were abused and overworked. One character, speaking of another's wife, said: "Treat her as a rational being, and my word for it, you'll have no more trouble."

Another: "Women have, or ought to have, as good a right to live as men."

46   Abigail had a good ear for emigrant speech. One character said:

"Well la bless us! If your mother hain't seed trouble enough to set the poor creetur crazy afore now; an' jist as she gits lifted up like, an' begins to think she can live easy, here comes this blow on her head."

Although many reviews mentioned its bad grammar, most of this was in dialog, and reflected the way pioneers actually talked. However, a few places show Abigail's lack of education, as when she wrote—not in dialog—"had awoke," and "cooks so good."

She herself later called the book an "indiscretion" that she produced when she "scarcely knew the rudiments of correct English speaking."

"I outgrew it before it reached the public eye," she said, and she would have suppressed it if she could.

Yet, for all its faults, *Captain Gray's Company* gave Abigail a lasting claim to fame. It was the first novel ever printed west of the Rocky Mountains.

A Speech and a Valentine

1860–1861

IN SPITE of the bad reviews, having a book in print made Abigail feel more independent. One day, in the *Argus*, she read about a meeting to be held in Lafayette, with Colonel E.D. Baker as speaker.

The colonel, who was campaigning for Lincoln, was a famous orator, and wherever he went the houses were packed, but only with men. Since he was an old friend of the Scott family from Illinois days, Abigail decided she was going to hear him talk. No matter that it was "improper" for women to go to political meetings. She was determined.

She persisted until good-natured Ben consented, and together they drove to town in the farm wagon, taking the children along just as if

Colonel E. D. Baker, a famous orator who campaigned for Lincoln. Wherever he spoke, houses were packed but ladies were not expected.

they were going to church on Sunday. First they went to the home of their friends, the J. R. McBrides.

"Eddie Baker is a wonderful speaker," Abigail insisted and explained that he had once been her father's partner in the sawmill business. 49

Mrs. McBride was doubtful. "Ladies are not expected," she said.

Abigail knew that quite well. She also knew that the man who was to introduce the speaker always told "dirty anecdotes," and that if she went, she might be insulted. But she talked so eagerly about the treat it would be to hear the famous colonel, and insisted so defiantly that women could enjoy a speech quite as much as men, that Mrs. McBride agreed to "face the storm."

That was encouragement enough for Abigail. From door to door she trudged, pleading with her friends. At last five others, making seven in all, agreed to attend the speech with their husbands.

Abigail's heart beat fast as she walked into the hall, her long dress sweeping the floor. Several hundred men had assembled. This was bold—unladylike. Hisses were clearly heard.

She pretended not to notice.

To her joy and relief, when E. D. Baker saw the ladies, he welcomed them and ordered a special place to be cleared for them near the platform. Skirt rustling, clinging to Ben's arm, Abigail took her seat.

She enjoyed every word of the speech. Abraham Lincoln had lived in the same county as the Scott farm in Illinois. It was thrilling to hear Colonel Baker, their mutual friend, talk about this railsplitter-farmer-lawyer who might be President of the United States. So this was the man's world, Jenny thought, the world of ideas. She'd enter it again, every chance she had, whether the ladies were expected or not.

After that, Jenny attended many meetings, and so did other women, including some who had been shocked when they heard about her first venture. She was becoming well known. Her name had often appeared in the paper. She was seen in public, along with her friends. Some people thought it was meddling for this blue-eyed young fireball to go poking her nose into places that "decent" women avoided. They blamed her for stirring things up.

One day while she was by the fireplace tugging at the dasher of a churn, Ben came in with

A drawing suggesting the sort of valentine
received by Abigail. The comic valentine
was seldom without a hint of cruelty.

the mail, which contained a large envelope.
Slitting it open, she found a comic valentine
that pictured a henpecked husband seated on a
chair, with squalling children clambering all

over him, and an irate, toothless, straggle-haired wife brandishing a broom. The verse was cruel.

52   *Fiend, devil's imp, or what you will*
        You surely your poor man will kill,
        With luckless days and sleepless nights,
        Haranguing him with Woman's Rights.

Abigail burst into floods of tears. "What have I done?" she wailed. "Did I ever give you or anybody else a reason for attacking me with a thing like this?"

"Never," Ben replied, looking up from his frolic with the children. "It was sent by a fool, as a joke. If I'd known what it was, or that you would care a rap about it, I wouldn't have brought it home."

Jenny wept and Ben comforted her, while the valentine lay on the floor beside them.

The Lucky Calamity

1861–1863

IT WAS 1861. Lincoln had been elected, the Civil War had begun, and Jenny was busier than ever, for she had a new baby boy, Wilkie.

One day in the spring she was picking ducks to get feathers for pillows, when a villager drove up in his carriage and met Ben at the woodpile. She overheard him asking Ben to be surety for a large sum, with interest at two percent per month, compounded. This meant that if the man couldn't pay off the notes, Ben would have to.

As the men strode into the house, Jenny tried to be silent. This was business, and women mustn't meddle. But it wasn't fair, she thought. She worked as hard as Ben. The decision should be partly hers.

Brushing the feathers off her hands and apron and leaving the duck securely pinioned, she went inside where Ben had already signed two notes and was ready to sign the third.

54   "My dear, are you quite certain about what you are doing?" she asked, leaning over his shoulder.

"Mama, you needn't worry," he replied. "You'll always be protected and provided for."

Although Abigail wanted to retort, "I guess I'll always earn all the protection I'll get," she bit her lips, remembered she was nothing in the eyes of the law, and returned to the duck.

Crops were good that year, and Ben proudly stored his wheat in a public warehouse in Lafayette, by the Yamhill River, expecting a fine price.

Autumn came. It snowed heavily in the mountains, then turned warm and cloudy. Day after day the rain poured down, while the snow pack melted, and all the streams ran bank full. Frightened, Abigail and Ben watched as the Yamhill River rose, threatening to wash away the warehouse where their precious crop was stored.

Still it rained. Families were driven from their homes. Men in boats rescued terrified people from upper windows. Towns were wiped out, fortunes lost. When she heard that the warehouse "was covered to the eaves," Jenny thought of the note Ben had signed, for the other man was facing ruin too.

The flood eventually subsided, but Abigail wrote in the *Oregon Farmer* that the wheat was ruined and the warehouse twisted until it looked "as if it had been built a hundred years ago." As she had feared, the man couldn't pay the notes, so they fell to Ben. In a desperate effort to get the money together, he went to work in the mines in eastern Oregon. But neither the mines nor the next fall's poor crop brought much of a return.

One day when Jenny had made "several rapid hurries down the hillside to scare the coyotes away from the sheep," the sheriff drove up just at dusk. Since Ben was absent, he served a summons on her for the amount of the notes.

Abigail was furious. To think that her consent hadn't been necessary—yet she could be held for the money! Controlling her anger, she took the warrant with a smile, and in her sweetest voice asked, "Won't you walk in?" The sheriff refused, for he had other papers to serve.

All afternoon as she bustled around the house, she composed triumphant speeches. During dinner she was pleasant, but when the hired man had gone, and Ben was playing with 56 the children, she told him what had happened. However, her well-planned phrases vanished, for he looked so pale and careworn that she couldn't say, "I told you so."

Ben could find only one way out, to sell the farm, salvage a team and wagon and some household goods, and move to Lafayette. Secretly Abigail was glad. She had often wished they were poor enough so she could live in town and take in boarders or washings.

Now they were that poor.

Ben's Accident
and What Happened Next

1863-1866

THE year they moved was 1863 and Abigail was twenty-eight. She had four children, Clara, Willis, Hubert and Wilkie, aged nine, seven, four and two. By now, the Civil War was half over. Although people in Oregon talked about the war, and some men joined the army, it was remote. To the young Duniways, their own problems were more pressing.

When they first moved to town, handsome, friendly Ben, who had always been his own master, went out every day to look for odd jobs. Generally he did hauling with his team and wagon. He was depressed at losing their farm, blamed himself, and began dickering to buy another, while Abigail planned to "help out" by opening a school for both boys and girls.

However, one day when they were "hardly settled in their new quarters," he was carried home, limp. His team had bolted, throwing him under the wheels, and his injuries were so severe that all their plans were upset.

58

Abigail pitched in, nursed Ben, tried to cheer him, and decided to expand her school. Since the loft of their cottage was unfinished, she lined and ceiled it with unbleached muslin, and used it as a dormitory for girls.

Her work load was crushing. She arose at three in summer, at four in winter, to clean and cook and wash and iron and make breakfast for her husband, children and boarders. When school began, at eight or nine, she had not had time to study any lessons, and she had to teach grammar, higher arithmetic, even algebra. Often she caught inspiration as she went along.

"Suppose we analyze it," she would say when the students (and perhaps the teacher too) were stuck.

She would use the windows, the stove, or any objects in the room as examples. If necessary, she would send a student to the black-

Portrait of Abigail as a young teacher, about the time they moved to Lafayette.

board, and while he or she struggled with the problem, Abigail at her desk would hastily read it through, think "like lightning" and figure it out.

60   The frail young woman who had formerly been so "ailing" didn't mind these long hours, for, she said, she could rest at her desk at the same time she was teaching the little ones; and the older ones were a stimulation.

"I led an easier life than I had known on a pioneer farm," she insisted. "Health improved, and hope revived."

Since Ben was never again able to do heavy work, their roles were reversed. He, a partial invalid, looked after the house and children. Abigail earned their living, an arrangement that suited her quite well. In fact, she believed that losing the farm saved her from an early death, like that of her mother.

Although a strange household for those times, theirs was a happy one. Ben didn't object to housework, and the children adored him. Neither he nor Abigail was a strict parent. The children were trained with gentleness, kindness, and reasoning, but all of them, especially Clara, received early responsibility.

In April, 1865, the new long-distance telegraph brought the joyful news that the Civil War was over, and five days later, word came of Lincoln's assassination. Abigail's brother Harvey, who by now was through college, wrote an editorial about it and soon became editor of the *Oregonian*, a fine newspaper. He had found his niche.

61

But Jenny was still searching for hers. The townspeople didn't quite accept these peculiar Duniways, with the mother who taught school while the father tended the babies and washed and ironed. Most villagers ignored them, and Jenny was lonely. She also discovered that a teacher's pay wouldn't support her family.

Jenny might be trapped in a bad situation, but she would never stay there long. In the summer of 1865 she took her brood to Albany, a larger town, on the Willamette River instead of a tributary. They probably made the move by river steamboat, a sixty-mile trip which would take two days, down the Yamhill, over the rapids, and then up the larger stream with the paddle wheel churning majestically.

In Albany Jenny bought a house with a workshop for Ben and a chicken house. She also built a small school, found a partner, and opened a millinery shop.

62

The house in Albany where the Duniways moved in 1865. Photographed in 1919.

Hats were generally handmade in those days, perky little bonnets loaded with veiling, ribbons, feathers, flowers and ruffles. They were fun to make, and expensive. As Jenny hoped, the shop prospered so well that after a year she 63 was able to give up her school.

But to have the handsome business she had in mind, she needed somehow to find more capital.

For Abigail, a need meant action. She dressed in her best, pinned on her hat, buttoned her gloves, and rode the bumpy stage to Portland. As she said:

"By the time I had moved my school house to Broadalbin Street and converted it into a store, with counters, shelves and show-cases, and had bought out a partner and was ready to start up with millinery and notions, I had left on hand, after paying expenses to Portland and return, just thirty dollars."

The Ladies' Underground

1866–1870

PORTLAND, the largest town on the Willamette, had eight thousand inhabitants who lived in small frame houses along a zigzag scattering of paths. Trees had been cut to make room for the town, jagged stumps stood everywhere, and a dark forest crowded in on three sides. Abigail swept down the board walks under the broad rooflike awnings, past the stores, saloons, and Chinese laundries, to the office of Jacob Mayer, wholesaler. Heart beating fast, she told him her story and asked for a stock of goods on credit for her millinery and notions store.

"Won't some of your friends go security for you?" he asked, not unkindly.

"My husband went broke going security, and

I vowed long ago that I would never copy his mistake," she replied with spirit.

"How much of a stock do you want?"

Abigail hesitated. She might as well ask for a lot. "About . . . about a hundred dollars will do for a beginning," she hazarded, her voice trembling.   65

Mr. Mayer chuckled. "Nonsense! You could carry home a hundred dollars' worth of millinery in a silk apron. Let me select you a stock of goods."

Humming, he bustled around his warehouse and laid out silk and feathers and artificial flowers until the bill totaled one thousand two hundred dollars.

Abigail looked longingly at it. "I'm afraid to risk it," she said, although she was tempted, for it would really make a fine shop. She offered him her thirty dollars in part payment.

Mr. Mayer refused. "Never mind. You'll need that money. Take this stock home and do the best you can with it. Then come back and get some more."

In three weeks she was back—with money to pay off her debt. This time she took three thousand dollars' worth of stock, again on credit, and again she soon paid it off. The Duniway store was underway.

Before long Abigail began to burn at tales her customers told.

66 One mother had been deserted by a husband who sold the household goods and left town. Now she had a chance to buy some furniture and rent a house cheaply.

"If I could borrow the money in a lump sum, I could repay it in installments," she said between sobs. "Then I could keep my children together, with the aid of a few boarders."

Later that day, when a friend dropped in, Abigail told him the story. "I'll loan her the money," he said heartily. "She can give me a chattel mortgage on the furniture."

As soon as she could leave the store, Abigail went to the meagre home with the good news, and before long the woman was established. All went well until the husband returned and rejected the mortgage—quite legally. The good friend was out his money. The woman sued for divorce. The home was broken up, children scattered.

It was wrong—wrong, thought Abigail. A woman's business should be her own. With laws as they were, a woman was at the mercy of her husband, and little more than a slave.

Another day, while Abigail was working on a twenty-dollar bonnet for a wealthy client, she looked out the shop window and saw a well-to-do farmer riding by on one horse, and proudly leading a fine racing animal which he had just 67 bought. He couldn't sit more erect, Abigail thought, if he'd swallowed a yardstick.

Sometime later his wife came in, followed by two little girls and carrying a baby in her arms.

"I've come to see if I could get a job of plain sewing," the mother said timidly. "I am obliged to earn some money."

"I'm sorry," Abigail replied, and explained that when she had extra work, she gave it to those in need.

Weeping, the woman said, "I promised these girls that if they would work hard and make lots of butter, I'd buy them waterproof suits to wear to Sunday school." Tears streamed down her face. "But *he* used the butter money to help pay for his new race horse."

"I'll sell you the goods and charge the bill to your husband," Abigail offered.

"John won't allow me to go in debt," replied the woman. Although Abigail offered to cut and fit the suits without charge, the woman refused, drew the blankets around the baby, and left.

Abigail sizzled. Women worked, just as men did. They ought to have some say in how the money was spent, some money of their own.

68 A year later, when the woman died, the minister preached a funeral sermon consoling the bereaved husband. Abigail thought long and deeply about the butter money, the "defrauded children," the dead wife, and the thoroughbred race horse.

Still again, a man came in with his wife and four little girls, and the mother selected four fashionable hats for them.

"What's the damage?" the man asked with gruff humor.

"Four hats at three dollars each, will be twelve dollars," Abigail replied.

The man's smile turned to a frown. He demanded something cheaper, and finally chose some bark hats which Abigail kept for berry pickers. The children were disappointed, and one said, "He thinks silver-mounted harness isn't a bit too good for his horses, though."

The mother silenced the child, smiled sweetly at her husband, and after sending him on an errand, had Abigail package the fashionable hats.

"When he comes back, he'll pay you the

price of the bark hats," she said, pulling some coins from her pocket. "Here's four dollars and a half. When I come to town again, I'll bring you the rest."

Abigail was puzzled. "Won't your husband notice the difference when he sees the hats?"

"No!" the woman replied sharply. "He doesn't know any more about a hat than I do about a horse collar!"

A few days later Abigail told another storekeeper about the hats. "Do you think I'll ever see the rest of the money?" she asked.

"Of course!" he replied with a chuckle. "We couldn't make any profit on fancy goods if it wasn't for what the women steal from their husbands."

Steal! From their husbands! Women were reduced to that! Abigail was aghast.

During their six years in Albany, Abigail bore two more sons, Clyde and Ralph. With one girl and five boys, the family was now complete. The pattern was still the same. Ben, with Clara's help, handled the house, and even invented a washing machine. Abigail earned the living.

Her shop became a center where women came not only to buy, but to talk with the

Abigail holding Clyde in 1867.

sympathetic Mrs. Duniway. She heard dozens of stories about injustice under the law, which she helped if she could. She lent goods to set up small shops, and at least once she lost her investment because the wife's business was 71 taken to pay an old debt of the long-absent husband, a debt incurred before marriage. She didn't dislike men. Quite the contrary, she had many men friends, and often persuaded them to help, too.

One day an acquaintance burst into her shop. "Mrs. Duniway!" she exclaimed. "I want you to go with me to the courthouse!"

"The courthouse is a place for men," Abigail replied. "Can't you get some man to go with you?"

"They all say they are too busy." The woman explained that her husband had died without a will, leaving it almost impossible for her to get enough of his estate to live on.

At first Abigail refused to go, but at last, half ashamed, she put on her hat.

"Only think!" said the woman as they hurried along the street. "My husband—if he had lived and I had died—could have spent every dollar we had earned in twenty years of married life, and nobody would have cared. My girls and I have sold butter, eggs, poultry, cord wood, vegetables, grain and hay—almost enough to pay the taxes and meet all of our bills, but I can't even buy a pair of shoe strings without being lectured by the court."

Abigail told the woman's story to the judge, who granted the immediate request, though he couldn't change the law. But back at the shop, while she worked on expensive bonnets for her well-to-do customers, she brooded. Unfairness again. Things ought to be changed.

That night at dinner she told her husband the story. "Ben, Ben," she said. "One-half of the women are dolls, the rest of them are drudges, and we're all fools!"

Ben, who was not feeling well that day, placed his hand on her head as she sat on the floor beside his couch. "Don't you know it will never be any better for women until they have the right to vote?" he gently asked.

"What good would that do?"

"Can't you see? Women do half the work. They ought to control half the pay," Ben replied. "If they voted, they would soon be lawmakers."

Abigail stared, feeling as if a light had been turned on. Lawmakers! If women could make the laws! Things could be changed! Maybe it was up to her to start something.

She thought of it as her "third birth."

73

CHAPTER TEN

Starting Something

1870–1871

THE first thing Abigail started was to talk with her good friends Martha Foster and Martha Dalton. Over the teacups, in November, 1870, when Abigail was thirty-six years old, these three formed the State Equal Suffrage Association.

Since she had to make a buying trip to San Francisco, the next thing Abigail started was to get herself appointed delegate to the California Suffrage Association, which was to meet there. She made the long trip alone, by the new train to Portland, then by steamer.

While in San Francisco she made a lively speech that was so well received she was offered a job lecturing at a set salary. Tempted, she wrote to Ben, and he replied with a telegram.

"Come home immediately. Business requires it."

Abigail might work for women's rights, but she also loved her family. She came home— after stopping at the offices of the *Pioneer*, a women's rights newspaper, and becoming its Oregon editor.

This really started something. Maybe, she thought, she couldn't take the job in California, because Ben and the children needed her at home. But a paper—that could be turned out anywhere.

Abigail was used to newspapers. Her brother Harvey was still editor of the *Oregonian*. Her oldest son Willis, age fifteen, had been working for two years as printer's devil in Albany, and the next two, Hubert, age twelve, and Wilkie, age ten, were newsboys. Ben could keep the house and look after the younger children. Clara, who was seventeen, could handle the shop. Maybe—just maybe . . .

Abigail was never one to let moss grow on a good idea. She returned from San Francisco on January 14. By May 5 she had moved her family to Portland, and the first issue of the new paper

The only picture of Ben and Abigail with the entire
family, taken in 1867. Standing, left to right, Hubert,
Willis, Clara, Wilkie. Seated, Ben, holding Clyde in his

lap, and Abigail. In the foreground is Ralph, taken from
another picture, carefully cut out and pasted in place,
probably by Abigail herself.

was on the streets. The *New Northwest* was its name. Under its masthead it carried the proud motto, "Free Speech, Free Press, Free People."

It hadn't been done without friction. Although Abigail generally had her own way, sometimes easygoing Ben set his heels and refused to budge—and one of those times was now. He was willing for her to have the paper, and willing to move, but he had seen enough of heavy debt.

"My husband," she said, "refused to put his signature to my papers; and I, being a wife, was legally dead and couldn't buy property in Portland."

Since they had recently sold their Hardscrabble farm for one thousand dollars, they had that much for a start. In addition Jenny borrowed some money on her own, bought a press and type, and found a house to rent for forty dollars a month. It was of two stories, wood frame, with room on the first floor for the notions and millinery shop, and two rooms on the second for the newspaper. She hired one Isaac Long, at twenty-five dollars per week, as foreman and typesetter, and put her sons to work helping Isaac. Ben himself got a light job at the customs house, so he could help with expenses.

A proud new editor. Abigail Scott Duniway holding the
first issue of *The New Northwest*.

But Jenny was so inexperienced that work-men took advantage of her. She spoke of "a nightmare of debt" and said that "men charged us what they pleased for labor and material and taught the tyros just such rules as suited them ... The expenses were double what they ought to have been."

By 1871 Portland had grown. It now had a telegraph to connect it with San Francisco, a line of horse-drawn streetcars, a stone post of-fice, and a steam ferry to East Portland. A few sidewalks and paved streets kept long skirts out of the mud, and oceangoing ships tied up at the wharves. At night oil lamps on poles cast flickering shadows across the theater, the ho-tel, and the saloons.

It also had three thriving daily papers to rival Abigail's weekly: the *Oregon Herald*; the *Port-land Daily Bulletin*; and brother Harvey's *Ore-gonian*. Although Harvey was a brilliant young editor, even for her first issue Abigail planned and managed her paper by herself, without ask-ing his advice.

The *New Northwest* was different from most crusading sheets, because Abigail was different from most crusaders. She was canny enough to include material that would appeal to every-

Downtown Portland looking as it did shortly after Abigail moved there.

one, and she wrote in a peppery style. Today, after a hundred years, the *New Northwest* is still fun to read.

On page one of her first issue, Abigail made a crashing start by an attack on three society women of Washington, D.C., who had protested against the women's rights movement. One of the three was Mrs. Henry Corbett, a Portland native, and wife of the Oregon senator.

Abigail said these three had no knowledge of the lives that humble women lived. She called them "parasites upon the country bounty who are flirting at the Capital." If they wanted to criticize women's rights, she said, they should first find out what it was like to be a worker.

She advised them, "Go home—from the Capital, from the society of gay women and worldly men; cease trying to outshine each other at receptions and soirees; lay aside flirtation and finery; take up the distaff and spin; grind corn at the mill; cook and wash and mend for your children—but do keep out of public life."

Since Senator Corbett was one of the most important men in Portland, the story rocked the town. A newspaper as reckless as that was sure to be read.

She had something for everyone.

In "Fashions for Ladies" she wrote, "The gypsy styles are all the rage. They are very becoming to youthful faces, and their neat and pretty trimmings help to freshen the features of the faded and careworn. Everybody should try to look as pretty as possible." 83

Claiming that men were really as vain as women, she quoted a men's fashion column. "The fronts of your coat skirts are to be cut away, displaying the matchless fit of the pantaloons."

In her advice column she suggested that Mary W. of Walla Walla might invest in a neat assortment of cheap jewelry, in which profits were good, and she advised Mrs. C. not to move to the city with four little boys.

She printed a poem by Julia Ward Howe and one by Bret Harte.

She promised a serial story beginning in the next issue.

And she supported women's rights, without making them a bore. A headline in the first issue was, "MRS. STEVENS' ACCOUNT OF A FINE IMPOSED UPON HER," which neatly combined a touch of gossip with the "cause."

When the paper was printed, Clara picked

the first issue from the press, and the boys took copies out to the streets.

Brother Harvey stopped in to congratulate her. Harvey opposed women's rights, but he knew good journalism when he saw it.

"You have made a capital paper," he said.

The Fight Begins

1871

WITHIN a month of the first issue of the *New Northwest*, Abigail started something else—the fight for equal suffrage, voting rights for women. To get it in Oregon, she thought, would take about five years.

Two famous suffragists, Susan B. Anthony and Elizabeth Cady Stanton, were lecturing in the West, so Abigail invited them to Portland for a series of talks, with herself as manager. As a further lure, she wangled free steamship tickets from California, but only Susan B. Anthony came.

Abigail had a prejudice against Miss Anthony, who had been pictured in the press as "cranky." Nevertheless, the first morning the great lady was in town, Abigail donned her best suit and hat, buttoned her gloves, picked up her umbrella, and went to Miss Anthony's hotel.

She was surprised at meeting a "soft-spoken, motherly-looking modestly attired woman" of about fifty years, to whom she "warmed instantly." Right from the start, they were friends, and Miss Anthony approved of Ben, too.

"Mrs. D. is a sprightly, intelligent, young woman," she wrote, and added, "Her husband—a sensible man—is proud that his wife possesses brains and self respect to use them."

Since the churches refused them a place to lecture, Abigail hired the Oro Fino Theater, and had her shop print programs decorated with scrolls and flowers. Ben collected the half-dollar admissions. Clara sang two songs, for which Abigail, of course, wrote the words.

She also introduced the speaker. Giving a lively talk to strangers in San Francisco had been easy enough, but this was her own home town.

"I went in fear and trembling before a cold, curious and critical crowd," she said.

However, although her voice "faltered," she was tall, imposing, and believed so earnestly in her cause that she was an instant success.

The famous American suffragist, Susan B. Anthony.

From that time on, she had more offers to speak than she could accept.

For more than two months Abigail traveled with Susan B. Anthony all over the Northwest, sometimes with Ben going along to keep track of details. They went up the Columbia on an elegant river steamer, taking Clara. The entire Duniway family went to the State Fair and camped in tents.

The two women went alone to hamlets of back country Oregon, riding fearlessly—and uncomfortably—by stagecoach, wagon, carriage, even by horseback, over sagebrush hills inland, or through dark forests along the coast. They went to Washington Territory and Canada. They spoke in churches if they were allowed to. Otherwise they accepted whatever was offered—a home, store, school, even a pool hall or saloon.

Wherever they went, they spoke of injustice. If a married woman happened to be injured in a railroad accident, she couldn't recover damages, but her husband could demand payment for loss of his wife's services. He could bind their children in apprenticeship, and the wife was powerless to prevent it. In Oregon, a society in which women held office could not be legally incorporated.

"In fact," Susan B. Anthony pointed out over and again, "married women are no more or less than slaves."

People were interested in this, so the audiences were generally large.

At the State Fair, speaking out-of-doors, they had to shout in order to be heard above the brass band, steam whistles, and cries of barkers. There Miss Anthony recognized a man in the audience.

"You!" she bellowed. "You wrote that article in Kansas, calling me a 'slab-sided old maid'!"

She then gave him a good-natured scolding that everyone except the unlucky man enjoyed.

At Umatilla Miss Anthony happened to meet the son of a New York friend. He had run away from home, and hadn't been heard of for years. When she talked kindly with him and urged him to get in touch with his family, he agreed.

"Some wine?" he said, offering her a glass, for he was now a bartender.

She accepted it graciously, took a polite sip, and handed it back. But the news of this "scandalous conduct" traveled fast. In Walla Walla, preachers used it as an excuse to deny them the use of churches. Nothing daunted, they used a saloon instead—which started a fresh batch of rumors.

In the saloon, men were drinking beer and spitting on the floor. Abigail glanced down. While the men watched in open-mouthed amazement, she lifted the edge of her trailing beruffled skirt, ripped off a ruffle, let it fall, looked again, and ripped off a second ruffle. It now cleared the mess on the floor.

"I tore that off for sanitary reasons," she stiffly explained.

Their reception varied. One newspaper said Miss Anthony's doctrines would bring "division in homes, anarchy in families and chaos in society." Another called her a "revolutionist," and said women's suffrage would "destroy all that is pure and beautiful in human nature."

At Port Gamble a wife invited them to her home, but the husband returned unexpectedly, treated them "like tramps," and ordered them out. Although Abigail wanted to stay and "conquer the head of the family," Miss Anthony hurried them to their hotel.

It was a lesson in publicity, for the story sped like a forest fire, and that night their audience was packed.

Part of the time, a woman named Mrs. J. Blakesley Frost also traveled in the Northwest, campaigning against them. As one newspaper put it, Mrs. Frost "went for the scalp" of Miss Anthony, and would "follow Miss Anthony's trail and shriek for men's rights."

This, the readers thought, was even better than a horse race. It fanned their interest.   91

The climax was at Olympia, Washington, where the territorial legislature invited Miss Anthony and Abigail to address a joint session. Until then it had been almost unheard-of for such a body to listen to woman speakers.

At last, in mid-November, they came home by stage from Olympia.

"The November rains had come," Abigail said. "The roads were horrible, and the night was pitch dark. But the driver was wise, the horses were intelligent, and we reached the Columbia River without other mishaps than bumps and bruises."

So the grand trip was over. Susan B. Anthony went back to California and then East, calling herself "as single-handed and penniless as usual."

As for Abigail, she had become a seasoned campaigner, no longer shaking with fright when she faced an audience. Glad to be home, she wrote an editorial for the *New Northwest*.

"Seated again at our little desk, scribbling

away at a rapid rate, while the click of falling type is heard within and pattering raindrops fall without, we feel that we would not exchange our office for a Dukedom or our editorial chair for the sole possession of the Isles of the Sea. And our fingers tingle with an electric glow that longs to turn itself into words of greeting to the many friends of our glorious cause who read the NEW NORTHWEST. To each and all of them we say, 'Thank God and take courage!! our cause is marching on!' "

Spearheading

1872–1876

ABIGAIL was a rocket. Lighted and off, she couldn't be stopped. Besides writing editorials, churning out one serial after another, canvassing for her paper, talking with women, ministers, judges, she now began to travel all over the Northwest. She gave lectures wherever she could get a hall—or a barn, saloon, stable, hotel, blacksmith shop. Often she slept in a one-room shanty, in a corner bed shared with two or more children; or she left by stage at night after her lecture in order to reach the next day's location.

Once, when she was speaking in a half-finished hotel dining room, the floor collapsed, dropping her listeners into the hole beneath. Undaunted, Abigail shouted, "Don't hurry, friends! Remain perfectly quiet and there will be no danger!" Within half an hour she had her flock gathered in another room, and resumed her lecture.

94   She became famous for her wit. While she was riding on a stage coach, one of the men passengers, slightly tipsy, began to jeer at woman suffrage.

"Madam," he said, "You ought to be at home, enjoying yourself, like my wife is doing. I want to bear all the hardship of life myself, and let her sit by the fire, toasting her footsies."

Later, when the stage let the man off at his own door, his wife was seen out at the wood-pile, chopping wood. Abigail leaned out the coach window and loudly called, "I see, my friend, that your wife is toasting her footsies! Goodbye!"

From that day on the poor man was nick-named "Old Footsie Toaster."

Again, a comic valentine was delivered to her on the platform. Opening it, she was shocked for a moment, but she turned it to face the audience and said, "The author of this ex-quisite piece of art didn't give his name, but he has sent along his picture." As the audience roared, she described the picture in detail, then continued, "I know the poor artist doesn't intend to represent my husband, for he isn't bald-headed."

Remembering the other valentine that had hurt her so, she told the audience about it and concluded, "Don't you see, ladies, that all we have to do, when we meet the nettle of ridicule, is to grasp it tightly, and then it cannot sting us too much."

In May, 1872, just a year after founding the *New Northwest,* Abigail went to the annual convention of National Woman Suffrage in New York, where she at last met the editor of the *Tribune,* Horace Greeley, who had been her girlhood ideal. He had recently been nominated as president of the United States, and she was delighted to be chairman of the committee which would interview him.

Knowing that Abigail had made a speech that morning in his favor, Greeley met them with a smile. But when she told him their errand, he brushed the fringes of his white whiskers, and in a voice "as hard as hailstones" said, "I don't want women to be men!"

Sharp-tongued Abigail had a lot to learn. "Neither do I!" she blurted, rising to her feet.

Horace Greeley, editor of the *New York Tribune* for over thirty years, and Abigail's girlhood ideal, although she could not avoid a fiery quarrel with him when they finally met.

"I wouldn't be a man if I could! And now, Mr. Greeley, mark my words; you'll never be president! You will find that women can tear down if they are not permitted to build up!"

Abigail was furious. She returned to the con- vention, stood up, and took back her speech of that morning, the one in which she had praised him. Even Greeley wasn't fit to be president, she thought, if he wouldn't support women's rights.

Later on, when she thought it over, she was appalled, for she knew she had behaved badly, that she should have flattered him and won him as a friend rather than stiffened his dislike. She wasn't a professional after all. Not yet.

Back home, she kept the *New Northwest* going. She printed methods "to keep clear of bed bugs" and "to keep flies out of butter." She offered advice on beauty and fashions:

"Freckles are produced by the breath of young men who indulge in the pernicious habit of smoking the vile compound known as cigarettes."

"The best bustles are stuffed with excelsior the same as furniture."

A reader asked, "Would I not run the risk of ruining my character by trying to engage in business? Men are so apt to talk about independent women." Abigail's reply was, "Tut! tut! Supose they do! They 'talk about' lazy women, idle women, expensive women, proud women, slatterns, wantons and prudes."

98   She sympathized with Mary E.S. because her husband, "an able-bodied healthy man, who is supported by her earnings at the wash tub," refused to carry the *New Northwest* home from the post office. She suggested to one young belle, "It is easier to get rid of him by a flat denial than by a promise of marriage." But to some mysterious request she snapped, "We cannot advise you. Ask your mother."

Abigail's serials included "Mrs. Hardine's Will," "Judith Reid, a Plain Story of a Plain Woman," "Judge Dunson's Secret," and dozens more—all bemoaning the woes of mistreated women. Hastily written though they were, they were lively and exciting, they held their readers—and promoted the cause.

She took potshots at other editors. "These truly deplorable specimens of humanity, whom we lately chastized into decency, have returned to their wallowing mire," and "Perhaps the editor was drunk again."

Even Harvey didn't escape. "We are sorry to see our Bible-adhering brother entangling him-

Harvey W. Scott at thirty-six, taken about 1873. He and
Abigail were friends, but that didn't alter the rivalry
between them.

self in such a fog. First he told us last week that Woman Suffrage was *right;* than he said it was *wrong* for married women because they were not free."

100   On the surface, Abigail and Harvey were friends. Big, handsome, looking like an outdoorsman, he was an editor of remarkable skill. Although he refused to have the *Oregonian* support her cause, he sometimes helped her get transportation to out-of-state meetings, and he printed articles about women who had been wronged. But the brainy brother and sister were far apart in beliefs about education and women's rights. Members of the family knew they had bitter quarrels.

Abigail was as fearless as she was witty. She had a guided tour of the "insane asylum", which in the main she approved, although she said, "It needs a woman physician."

She exposed the Multnomah County Courthouse Ring, the "Schoolbook Fraud", and the refusal of the school at Forest Grove to admit a student who was illegitimate.

She won a law suit when a rival named his paper the *Northwest News,* a name so much like hers that he collected some of her accounts.

All this made her paper talked about and brought subscribers. It also made it possible for her to move out of the rented house and buy a fine large one with high steps, bay windows, gingerbread trim. And the Duniways' first in- door plumbing.

Even so, the financial road wasn't easy. Abigail gave premiums to those who brought in subscriptions, such as a reed organ for seventy-five or a sewing machine for fifty. For bringing in two the lucky winner could choose a pair of marble vases, or half a dozen ivory napkin rings, a spangled lady's fan, kerosene lamp, teapot or birdcage.

Repeatedly she pleaded for her readers to pay up their accounts, so she could pay hers, and she added to her income by innumerable lectures. In 1873, illness in the family caused her to cease publication for two months. And still, by the time the paper had been operating for six years, she had brought the "nightmare of debt" down to one hundred and six dollars.

In 1876 Abigail took another long trip, to the Centennial Exposition in Philadelphia, starting out blithely on a Columbia River steamboat with twenty-five dollars in her pocket. A fellow-passenger, shocked at her finances, got per-

The house on Fifth and Clay in Portland which Abigail and Ben bought in the mid-1870s and in which she lived until her death. It became famous as a center for the women's suffrage movement.

mission from the captain for her to speak on shipboard and take up a collection. It was eighty-seven dollars. She made other speeches, too, going ashore when the ship tied up, and acquiring such a surplus that she wired some of it back home.

Part of this trip was on narrow-gauge construction tracks, laid for building a stretch of railroad. Cattlemen, angry because the right-of-way cut through their range, would often put dead cattle on the tracks, so the railroaders had taught a little dog to go on ahead.

"The faithful animal," Abigail said, "never failed to give us warning in time to avoid a wreck."

She was away several months this time, for she campaigned in Washington and Idaho on her way back. While she was stumping the country, Ben was busy too, helping with the house and working at his job at the U. S. Customs Office.

Clara, twenty-two by now, had heavy responsibility, for little Ralph was only seven, and Clyde was ten. Besides looking after them and assisting Ben with the cooking and cleaning, Clara managed the notions and millinery shop, as she had ever since the family moved to Portland.

Through all the years while Abigail was teaching and working for women's rights, Clara had stood loyally by, singing for meetings, helping in the home and shop. But now she 104 rebelled. During her mother's absence, the girl ran away and married a young man named Don Stearns. This was a blow for Abigail, but she didn't forget that she loved her daughter. When she returned from her long trip, she had a big party for the young couple, and she and Clara remained friends.

Even though Abigail was gone so much, their home was happy and she was important to it. Ben and the children always welcomed her eagerly when she returned after her daily rounds, and she would entertain them in the evening with hilarious tales of people she had met.

It was a free, friendly relationship. "B.C." and "Jenny with the Nut-Brown Hair" were the names the children called them. As "Jenny" she would vigorously pump the reed organ, playing and singing their favorite tunes.

A frog who would a-wooing go, she sang, or *Oh, where have you been, Billy boy, Billy boy, Oh, where have you been, charming Billy?* Or, *Listen to the patter of the sweet rain on the roof.*

A portrait of Clara, done around 1878, shortly after her marriage.

Jenny loved the world, but she loved her home and family too, and Ben and the children listened in delight.

106

Problems and Progress

1876–1883

GENERALLY Abigail defended herself by her wits. She could be really funny, and she often said that women could never win votes by antagonizing men.

Taunted because she didn't stay home and keep house, she said she had made enough butter "to grease the axles of creation."

She told a male heckler, "I've always heard the difference between a man and a mule was that a man could change his mind."

However, any reformer makes enemies, and so did she. Some didn't want to lose their male privileges. Others thought women didn't know enough to vote, or that voting women would lose interest in their homes. Often her most rabid enemies were women themselves, who considered her cause "unladylike." Jenny herself sometimes added to the ill will by speaking out so bluntly.

Wild stories were told—that she was a "free lover," a drunkard, that she met men in hotel rooms, gave away her children, whipped Ben, and carried a cane. Once, on a river steamship, a fellow-passenger, not realizing who she was, said to her, "And in Oregon, I am told, you have that horrid woman, a Mrs. Duniway, who drinks, and smokes and swears like a man."

In one town she was met with "showers of eggs," and the sheriff had to call out a posse to protect her. Then, she said, "I shook the dust of the town from my feet and departed in a closed carriage."

One Sunday morning at breakfast Willis glanced at a rival newspaper, turned pale, and handed it to Hubert. Without a word the two got up and left the room, taking the paper. Alarmed, Abigail followed them to the door and pleaded with them not to do anything rash, but they strode away. The next she heard of them, they had been arrested for assault and battery and released on ten-thousand-dollars bail, put up by a friend.

She didn't leave any record of what the article had said about her, but it was serious enough to keep the newspaper out of the mails, and the next morning's *Oregonian* carried a "blistering editorial" in her defense. Even the prosecuting attorney told the sons, "Stay with it, boys. You did exactly right!"

When Abigail first came to Oregon she had worked in her father's Temperance Hotel. For many years she supported the temperance movement, which originally aimed for self-control, especially control over drinking habits. Abigail said she favored moderation in all things—including "woe, want, waste, poverty, excessive riches, murder, arson, slander, fever, contagion, lust, covetousness, drunkards, gluttony, lying, robbery, cruelty, and theft."

As time went on the women's movement was joined by prohibitionists and the WCTU (Women's Christian Temperance Union) who wanted to stop all sale of liquor. This, Abigail thought, was a thrust in the opposite direction from hers. Women's rights were toward freedom. Prohibition was away from freedom.

Actually no easy course was open. If she supported prohibition, most men would vote against her. If she rejected it, she would lose the help of the WCTU. She and her sons were

Voters' Book of Remembrance.

Voters of Portland, The Book of Remembrance is this day opened, and you are called upon to choose "whom ye will serve." On one hand are found prostitutes, gamblers, rumsellers, whiskey topers, beer guzzlers, wine bibbers, rum suckers, hoodlums, loafers and ungodly men. On the other hand are found Christian wives, mothers, sisters and daughters of the good people of Portland. You cannot serve two masters. You must be numbered with one or the other. Whom will ye choose?

Remember the Temperance ticket. Vote for it early and work for it earnestly all day. It is the safe side.

Remember that this is a struggle between virtue and vice. May you be found on the side of virtue.

Remember that the success of either of the other tickets is the success of whiskey—supported by bad men and polluted women.

Remember that the whiskey advocates employ prostitutes to insult Christian women while praying and reading the Holy Bible.

Remember that the police of Portland arrest, fine and imprison the Christian women of Portland for reading the Bible and praying.

Remember that the police of Portland are devoted to the protection of prostitution, drunkenness and debauchery and the persecution and punishment of virtue.

Remember that persons are known by the company they keep. Birds of a feather flock together.

Remember that R. R. Thompson, one of the whiskey candidates on one of the whiskey tickets, served on the jury that fined and imprisoned Christian women in Portland for reading the Bible and praying.

Voters' Book of Remembrance. Propaganda from the WCTU.

all teetotalers, but she did as she thought right, and withdrew her support from the temperance movement.

However, she still wanted to speak on women's rights at temperance meetings, which made the leaders furious. One evening a choir of ladies started singing every time Abigail stood up. She then said, "Let us pray," and delivered a twenty-minute speech in the form of a prayer, which no one dared interrupt.

One speaker, the Reverend I. D. Driver, blared, "I charge the sins of the world upon the mothers of men. There are twenty thousand fallen women in New York—two million of them in America. We cannot afford to let this element vote!"

Jumping to her feet, the enraged Abigail shook her finger at him. "How dare you make such charges against the mothers of men! What about fallen men . . . I pronounce your charge a libel on womanhood, and I know that if we were voters, you would not dare to utter it!"

At another meeting, when the leaders accepted all delegates except Abigail's, whom they called "setting hens," and "belligerent females," Abigail moved to admit her group, and refused to back down. After some sharp words, the chairman ordered, "Take that crazy woman out of the house and take care of her."

Abigail was tall for her day and impressive. The officer who tried to evict her "quailed" before her uplifted pencil, while men nearby began taking off their coats to defend her. Such pandemonium followed that it took until one o'clock the next afternoon to get things quieted down enough to vote—and her group received seats. "My hand was so often and enthusiastically shaken," she said, "that my shoulder was severely lamed."

In spite of the opposition, the movement for women's rights was gaining ground, especially in the states of the West. Wyoming had been the first to grant woman suffrage, away back in 1869. In 1874, Oregon had passed the Married Woman's Property Bill which forbade a husband's creditors seizing his wife's tools, furniture, or stock in trade.

In 1883, twelve years after Abigail started her newspaper, the legislature of Washington Territory, where she had often lectured, was considering a bill to grant women the right to vote. Naturally, Abigail was on hand for the final roll call, sitting in the council room, amid "death-like stillness" as the members shouted

An engraving of Abigail done in 1876, bearing the slogan "Yours for Liberty" in her hand.

their "aye," or "no." She kept her own tally. When the deciding "aye" was cast, she rushed to the telegraph office to wire the result to her paper. Although the *New Northwest* had gone 114 to press, her sons opened the forms and inserted the news, and in half an hour newsboys were crying the victory through the streets.

As Abigail hurried home, she had rosy dreams. Largely through her work, the people of Oregon (meaning the men) were about to vote on woman suffrage. With Washington in the fold, she thought, surely her own state would follow.

Surely the great day of freedom for Oregon women would soon be here.

The Darkest Years

1 8 7 3 – 1 8 9 6

AS 1883 opened, Abigail's personal life was smooth. She had a new book in print, a story told in verse and entitled *David and Anna Matson.* Three sons, Willis, Hubert and Wilkie, were partners in the paper, and daughter Clara was still living nearby.

Abigail herself was receiving national recognition. Proudly she reprinted in the *New Northwest* a letter from Lucy Stone of the national committee: "I have ... rejoiced ... over the result in Washington Territory, and in my heart congratulated *you* who have so long ... borne the heat and burden of this great strife." With Oregon soon to vote on her "cause," Abigail felt her great goal was within reach.

However, she hadn't reckoned with men's

belief that women's votes would cost them their beer. The bill lost.

She was nearly fifty years old, growing stout, with her hair brushed until it shone and pulled back into a tight knot. Undaunted, she turned to her typewriter, and prepared to carry on the fight.

And then Clara fell ill with tuberculosis. For three years Abigail grieved as her daughter went slowly downhill, until, in January, 1886, Clara died, only thirty-one years old.

"I wish I could go with you, darling," Abigail murmured, on Clara's last day.

"You must stay to finish your work, Ma," the young woman replied.

Even though Abigail may have imposed on Clara by giving her so much care of the house and shop, she loved the girl with all her heart and was desolate. "I pressed onward as before," she said, "losing my sorrow, as best I could, in pursuit of my unfinished work."

Since spiritualism was a popular belief at that time, Abigail tried to find comfort in it. Later, writing of Clara, she said, "She passed away in January, 1886, but I heard from her, through private psychic sources, within a month; and I have never since been able to think of her as dead."

This was only the beginning. For the rest of the year everything seemed to fall apart.

Ben was seriously ill. He and Abigail thought they could make their fortunes by buying cheap land where the railroad was to pass 117 through Idaho, and he was advised that outdoor living might improve his health. So he and several of their sons left Portland by boxcar, with Ben riding on a stretcher at one end of the car, while their animals and goods rode at the other.

Abigail was alone in the big house.

The women in her cause were quarreling among themselves, and some turned against her.

When Washington became a state instead of a territory, the new constitution "shut down the iron gates in the women's face—leaving them ex-voters." The state of Washington canceled woman's suffrage, mainly because men were afraid women would vote for prohibition.

With her husband and sons moved away, Ben ill, her daughter gone, her crusade crumbling, Abigail was sad and weary. She thought the "cause" would fare better without her, and she longed for rest. So in 1887 she sold her paper to the same *Northwest News* that she once had sued. She then followed her family to Idaho, where she found Ben feeling better.

Abigail's sons grown to manhood, around 1900. From left to right: Hubert, Clyde, Ralph, Willis and Wilkie.

Although she expected to live quietly on his farm, Idaho was also struggling for women's rights, and its workers soon called on the famous Oregon editor for help. Shaking off her blues, Abigail picked up her umbrella, and for the next seven years she traveled over the state, made speeches, and visited the legislature. Since she still owned the big house in Portland, she spent her winters there, writing. Often, to help out the family budget, she took in boarders, but reluctantly.

"I don't like work in that line one whit better than my sons do," she said.

Ben, too, was occasionally back and forth between the two states.

By 1894 it was all too clear that the Idaho venture wasn't going to make their fortune after all, because the railroad was delayed, and wouldn't have come through in time to help them. Since Ben was worse again, and Portland was home, the Duniways moved back to Oregon.

Still active, wanting to write, Abigail took on a new job as editor of the *Pacific Empire,* a handsome magazine that was backed by other suffragists. Here she didn't have to worry about subscriptions and advertisers. Instead she spent all her time writing editorials, news, and serials, and supporting her favorite cause.

Woman's suffrage in the West continued to grow. Wyoming and Colorado adopted it. In 1896 Idaho and Utah followed suit, these four being the only states where women could vote.

120

In June of that year Abigail promoted a convention of women's clubs, called a "Women's Congress," in Portland. She kept her family busy. Willis spoke the first evening, Hubert the second, while Hubert's wife was in charge of all the music. It was a great success.

But after that Abigail gave up writing for the *Pacific Empire,* for Ben was seriously ill.

"Good night, Mother," he told her one night. "You must have some rest. Don't worry. We'll meet again in the morning."

That wasn't to be. On August 6, 1896, the magazine contained a simple notice written by Abigail herself, saying that Ben had died. "A good man who is gone," she called him.

Harvey's paper, in a long column about Ben, spoke of his truth and honor, his kindness of heart. "In all his life," it said, "he never did an unworthy act."

In the next issue Abigail herself had more to say. She reminded her readers of the early persecution of suffragists, and Ben's loyal help over all the years. "He never lost faith," she said. "The women of Oregon owe him a debt of gratitude which cannot be expressed in words."

Now Abigail was alone.   121

The Grand Old Lady
of Oregon

1896–1915

IN spite of her grief, Abigail was soon battling
again. She made speeches, organized groups,
spoke to the state legislature, tried to channel
the new women's club movement into suffrage. She was especially proud that Idaho,
where she had campaigned so long, now allowed its women to vote.

"The eyes of the world," she said, "are on
these states of the Pacific Northwest."

She went to two national conventions as
honored speaker, to Grand Rapids, Michigan,
in 1899; to Washington D.C. in 1900.

Her tongue was still tart.

"Show me a woman who doesn't like men

and I will show you a sour-souled, vinegar-vis-aged specimen of unfortunate humanity," she said in Grand Rapids, "and the very best thing she could do for her country would be to steal away and die, in the company of a man who doesn't like women." 123

She spoke of woman at the kitchen sink, at which she had always been "protected" (without wages), and "at the cooking stove, the rolling pin, the wash tub and the ironing board, at which she has always been shielded (without salary)."

"We will never get the ballot till the crack of doom if we persist in demanding it as a whip," she said. "To win men's votes for the cause, make him laugh . . . Impress on him: we are not intending to interfere, in any way, with his rights."

She had come a long way from the skinny girl who taunted her hungry Uncle Levi, or the earnest young woman who told Horace Greeley he could never be president.

In 1900 Abigail managed to bring suffrage to a vote by the people of Oregon. It lost, but by a narrow margin, and Abigail always thought the loss was due to Harvey, for he and his powerful paper had come out strongly against her. This infuriated Jenny. She went to Harvey and "had it out" with him. She also wrote to Clyde about the "humiliation and shame of my brother's nefarious conduct" and said, "We would have won triumphantly if the *Oregonian* had not stirred up the slum and slime of the city's purlieus."

124

Harvey and Jenny were much alike—smart, determined, outspoken. She burned at women's wrongs and was sure suffrage was the way to mend them. He was equally sure that ignorant voters would be dangerous—and most women weren't educated. She scorned him as an old fogey. He was embarrassed at her "antics." Inevitably, they collided so violently that in their later years they refused to sit at the same table.

Abigail was sixty-six now, but she fought doggedly on. She defied Harvey. "It is too late in my career for him to stop it with anything but a bullet." She sent out a telegram through the Associated Press, "Defeated, but not beaten! . . . Going right ahead. Will win next time." She planned to make another attempt at once, but was stopped by a serious mastoid infection, and without her the campaign folded.

By 1904 Oregon had a new law that allowed the people to vote on any measure, provided enough of them signed a petition. Abigail and her workers secured the signatures but didn't have them certified in time to get their law on the ballot. However, almost everybody had heard of her. In the state where she had once been hated and feared, she was now called "the Grand Old Lady of Oregon."

She published another book, *From the West to the West: Across the Plains to Oregon*. Like *Captain Gray's Company*, it was fiction based on her own experiences as an emigrant. Some of it touched on the death of her Uncle Lindsey so long ago at the hands of a mob.

That same year, 1905, when the Lewis and Clark Exposition was held in Portland, one day of it was "Abigail Scott Duniway Day." Bands played. Crowds cheered. Abigail, naturally, made another speech. She had high hopes that the next vote for women's suffrage in 1906 would pass.

She had proudly invited the national leaders of the suffrage movement to have their own convention in Portland, because she wanted them to see the progress Oregon was making. Now she found out that the invitation was a mistake. Although Susan B. Anthony herself left, some of the others were so impressed that they decided to stay right there and take charge of the promising campaign.

"The Grand Old Lady of Oregon." A portrait of Abigail done around 1905.

Oregon
Equal Suffrage Association

Representing the National American Woman Suffrage

President—REV. ANNA H. SHAW

Recording Secretary—ALICE STONE BLACKWELL

Corresponding Secretary—KATE M. GORDON

Chairman Press Work
MRS. IDA PORTER BOYER

Auditors LAURA CLAY
        DR. ANNICE JEFFREY MYERS   Lock Box 200, Portland

State Headquarters 410, 411 and 412 Stearns Bldg., 6th and Morrison Sts.

PORTLAND, OREGON, MAY 16, 1906.

Dear Friend:

We believe that the mothers, wives, sisters, and daughters of Oregon are as intelligent and patriotic as the women of Idaho, Colorado, Utah, Wyoming, England, Scotland, Ireland, Canada, Norway, Australia, New Zealand, or any other place where women now vote.

We earnestly appeal to every liberty-loving man in Oregon who believes in a square deal and fair play for all to prove his faith in the mothers and wives of Oregon by placing an X between 302 and YES on his ballot June 4th. Let Oregon lead the march of progress on the Pacific Coast.

Yours for justice,

ABIGAIL SCOTT DUNIWAY,
    Honorary President Oregon Equal Suffrage
    Association and State Federation of Woman's
    Clubs.

MRS. HENRY WALDO COE,
    President Oregon Equal Suffrage Association.

CHARLOTTE M. CARTWRIGHT,
    President Woman's Pioneer Auxiliary Ass'n.

SARAH A. EVANS,
    President Oregon Federation of Woman's Clubs.

ESTHER C. POHL, M.D.
    President Woman's Medical Association.

A letter from the Oregon Equal Suffrage Association.

This alarmed Abigail, so she resigned as state president, leaving the field to the national leaders. As she feared, they and the WCTU joined forces.

128   It won't work, she thought. If the women said, "Give us the ballot and we'll put down your whiskey," the men would reply, "Very well, we won't give you the ballot and that will settle it."

The women in charge of the campaign didn't listen to her, and the measure was defeated. Even so, Harvey's *Oregonian* paid her a surprising tribute.

"The agitation was begun by Mrs. Duniway and has been due to her, more than to all other agencies together . . . The progress it has made is an extraordinary tribute to one woman's energy."

In 1908, Abigail returned to the battle and personally borrowed five hundred dollars to pay the cost of petitions. She lost. In 1910, the voters again soundly rejected the movement. Undaunted, Abigail wouldn't give up, and year by year her support grew. The big house, where she still lived, became famous as a center for women's suffrage.

By 1912 the "five-year fight" had stretched to

WOMEN
PAY TAXES!!
WOMEN
OBEY THE LAWS!

Women and Children suffer from dirty streets, impure milk, adulterated food, bad sanitary conditions, smoke laden air, underpaid labor.

WOMEN CLEAN THE HOMES:
LET THEM HELP CLEAN THE CITY

VOTE | **300 X 'YES'** | **AMENDMENT NO. 1,** NOV. 5, 1912

It will give the women A SQUARE DEAL.
It will give your girl the same chance
as your boy.

VOTES FOR WOMEN

COLLEGE EQUAL SUFFRAGE LEAGUE, 406 SELLING BLDG.

A pro-Suffrage poster, 1912.

forty-one. Although Abigail was seventy-eight, frail, and often too ill to make speeches, she continued to write, and again she borrowed money to pay for petitions. She became a symbol of the struggle, her home was decorated with "suffrage yellow" bunting, and on her birthday she was honored by a huge party attended by Oregon's great, including the governor himself. Once more she was in the thick of things.

She and her co-workers sent speakers in the fascinating new automobiles all around town to give short talks. They had a float in the Rose Festival Parade, winning a silver loving cup which they presented to her on the porch of her home. They put up posters showing Oregon as the only state on the Pacific which hadn't given women the vote, for by now the others had done so. A popular actress handed out sandwiches from a truck. Brother Harvey had recently died, and this time the powerful *Oregonian* was on her side.

On election day men marched to the polls. Although most of Abigail's workers were wildly excited, that night while votes were being counted, she went to bed early. The reason? She wanted to be fresh in the morning, so

130

if the bill failed, she could start another campaign at once.

But the next day she was awakened by drum and fife leading a suffrage demonstration. The bill had passed, 61,265 to 57,104.

Abigail still had one more moment of drama. The governor of Oregon, Oswald West, remembered a day at the State Fair when he was only a ten-year-old boy. Seeing a crowd, he had crossed the street barefoot, straw hat in hand, and found a seat on one of the rough planks down front. Abigail, then a handsome crusader, was giving a speech.

"Don't you consider your mother as good, if not better, than an ordinary Salem saloon bum?" she had shouted, happening to look his way.

Young Oswald, who had often seen the saloon bums in the livery stable, replied under his breath, "Sure I do." He never forgot the incident, which he later said had colored his whole political life.

Now one of his duties was to issue a proclamation that would add the Equal Suffrage Amendment to the Oregon Constitution. Remembering the fiery lady of long ago, he asked Abigail to prepare the document for him to

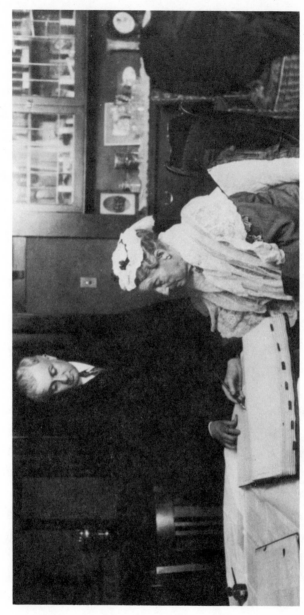

A proud Oregonian registers to vote. Abigail, shown here with Multnomah County Clerk John B. Coffey, registers after suffrage amendment was adopted, 1912.

Abigail Scott Duniway, first woman at the polls.

133

sign. She did it, "in a proud but trembling hand," the first time such an important paper had been entrusted to a woman. It was signed and sealed in her presence, after which Governor West gave her one copy and filed another. He also arranged to let her become the first woman to vote in all the state.

134

Still the "Grand Old Lady of Oregon," Abigail lived on in the big house. All her sons were successful, in business, in the law, one as president of the University of Montana. A year after the triumph of her "cause" she met sorrow again, for Willis, the oldest one, died, so respected that some thought he might well have become governor of the state. Two years after that, on October 11, 1915, Abigail herself died, age eighty-one.

Today Duniway Park and Duniway School in Portland honor her memory. Her name is inscribed on a bronze plaque in the League of Women Voters' Hall of Fame, and many books about woman's rights describe her achievements. In World War II a large landing craft was named for her.

During her last years she spent her time writing *Path Breaking*, a rambling but never dull autobiography. One granddaughter re-

PATH BREAKING

AN AUTOBIOGRAPHICAL HISTORY
OF THE EQUAL SUFFRAGE
MOVEMENT IN PACIFIC
COAST STATES.

BY
ABIGAIL SCOTT DUNIWAY

Abigail Scott Duniway, Signing Oregon's Equal Suffrage Proclamation, in
Presence of Governor Oswald West and Mrs. Viola M. Coe

Frontispiece and title page of *Path Breaking*, the book Abigail wrote about
the Suffrage Movement toward the end of her life.

135

membered her as a doll-like little old lady in a lace cap and fichu, banging industriously on a typewriter and wielding an enormous pair of shears. Sometimes she sat up in bed and balanced the typewriter on her knees.

Near the end of her book, Abigail spoke of the duties of women, especially of the lucky ones who could go to college. To receive favors, she thought, is an obligation, not a right. For the last words of *Path Breaking* she wrote:

"The debt that each generation owes to the past it must pay to the future."

It summed up her life.

Bibliography

PRIMARY SOURCES

Douthit, *Souvenir of Western Women*, Portland, 1905

Duniway, Abigail Scott *From the West to the West*, Chicago, 1905 (autobiographical fiction)

Duniway, Abigail Scott *Narrative*, in Scott, *History of Oregon*, Vol. III Cambridge, 1924

Duniway, Abigail Scott *Captain Gray's Company*, Portland, 1859

Duniway, Abigail Scott *Personal Reminiscences of a Pioneer*, in Gaston, *History of Portland*, Vol. III, Portland, 1912

Duniway, Abigail Scott *Path Breaking*, Portland, 1914 (her autobiography)

Bailey, Margaret J. *Grains or Passages in the Life of Ruth Rover, with Occasional Pictures of Oregon, Natural and Moral,* Portland, 1854

Gaston, Joseph *Portland: Its History and Builders.* 4 volumes. Portland, 1912

138 Scott, Harvey *History of the Oregon Country.* 6 volumes. Cambridge, 1924. Mainly reprints from the *Oregonian.* Compiled by his son.

Victor, Frances Fuller *All Over Washington and Oregon,* San Francisco, 1872

Geneological Forum of Portland, Oregon, Compilers and Publishers, *Index to Oregon Donation Land Claims,* 6 volumes, Portland, 1957–1975

SECONDARY SOURCES

Harper, Ida *History of Woman Suffrage,* Vol. III, about 1922

Harper Ida *The Life and Work of Susan B. Anthony,* Indianapolis, 1899

Powers, Alfred, *History of Oregon Literature,* Portland, 1935

Laver, James *Costume Through the Ages,* New York, 1963

Richey, Elinor *Eminent Women of the West,* Berkeley, 1975

Ross, Nancy W. *Westward the Women*, New York, 1944

Yamhill County Historical Society, *Old Yamhill*, Lafayette, 1976

Smith,   Helen   Krebs *The   Presumptuous   139 Dreamers*, Vol. I, Portland, 1974

PERIODICALS

American Mercury, August, 1948, *No Doll Was Abigail*, by Sibyl Walker

Daily Oregon Bulletin (Morning Bulletin)— several issues, 1871

The *New Northwest*, Abigail Scott Duniway, editor. Microfilm. Published Portland, 1871–1887

The *Oregon Argus*, W.A. Adams, editor. Microfilm. Published Oregon City, 1855–1860

Oregon Historical Quarterly, December, 1949. *Reminiscences and Anecdotes* by Oswald West.

The *Oregonian*—published Portland—many scattered items.

The *Pacific Empire*, Abigail Scott Duniway, editor. Portland, 1895–1897

Western Lady—One clipping. 1906? *How I Be-*

came a Literary Lady, by Abigail Scott Duniway. From a scrapbook.

MANUSCRIPTS

140 Capell, Letitia Lee, *Biography of Abigail Scott Duniway,* Master's thesis, University of Oregon, Eugene, June, 1934. (Includes interviews with Duniway family members, Abigail's son and daughters-in-law.)

Material from David Duniway, family papers, scrapbooks, letters

Records of land sales at Clackamus County Courthouse.

Roberts, Leslie McKay, *Suffragists of the New West: Abigail Scott Duniway and the Development of the Oregon Woman Suffrage Movement.* B.A. thesis, Reed College, May, 1969. Partly based on extensive collection of Duniway family letters.

Scrapbooks at Oregon Historical Society

The Trail Diary Abigail Scott, crossing to Oregon, 1852. Microfilm

U.S. Land Office Abstracts of Oregon Donation Land Claims, 1852–1903. Reel 4, Vol. 8— Microfilm

Interviews: David Duniway
　　　　　　 Elesa Scott Keeney

Index

146

Photo Credits

"I tore that off for sanitary reasons." (p. 90) from
The Presumptuous Dreamers
by Helen K Smith, by courtesy of
Smith, Smith and Smith Publishing Company.

"in a proud but trembling hand," (p. 131) quoted by Oswald West
in the *Oregon Historical Quarterly*, Dec. 1949, p. 248.
Used by permission of the Oregon Historical Society.

The portrait of John Tucker Scott and the picture of the Scott farm
in Illinois are from Scott, Harvey W. *History of the Oregon Country*,
vol. III. Cambridge: Riverside Press, 1924.
Courtesy of Elesa Scott Keeney and Harvey Scott.

Quotes from the "Trail Diary" and letters and the pictures
on pages 4, 15, 17, 20–21, 34, 59, 62, 70, 76–77, 79, 102, 105, 113, 118,
126 courtesy of David Duniway.

The pictures on pages 24, 25, 37, 40–41, 51, 81, 87, 96, 99, 110, 127,
129, 132, 133, 135 courtesy of the Oregon Historical Society.

The Author

Dorothy Morrison spent her childhood in Nashua, Iowa, and attended the University of Northern Iowa and the State University of Iowa, where she received a bachelor's degree and did one year of graduate work in music. After two years of teaching, she married Dr. Carl V. Morrison, and moved to Portland, Oregon.

She has played violin with community orchestras, chamber groups, and the Portland Opera Orchestra, and is presently a member of the Chehalem Symphony Orchestra. Her other hobbies include photography, travel, needlework, square dancing, and most recently, swimming with the Master's Swimming Program. She has traveled extensively in Mexico, Europe and the South Pacific.

With special interest in the history of the Northwest, she collects original books on that period. She is coauthor with Dr. Morrison of *Can I Help How I Feel?*, which deals with emotional problems of young people. She has also written three other biographies related to the West:

The Eagle and the Fort: The Story of John McLoughlin, Chief Sarah: Sarah Winnemucca's Fight for Indian Rights, Under a Strong Wind: The Adventures of Jessie Benton Frémont.

Following the death of Dr. Morrison in 1980, Mrs. Morrison married Robert C. Hunter, an attorney. They live on a forty-acre farm west of Portland.